Life II

V. YOUNG

authorHOUSE®

AuthorHouse™
1663 Liberty Drive
Bloomington, IN 47403
www.authorhouse.com
Phone: 1 (800) 839-8640

Published by AuthorHouse 04/10/2018

ISBN: 978-1-5462-3562-0 (sc)
ISBN: 978-1-5462-3563-7 (e)

Put Yourself First! I used to think that was a selfish way of thinking, but not anymore. My reasoning changed because I learned that if you don't put yourself first, and do what you have to do for you, then eventually, you won't be able to do for anybody else. So take care of yourself, and make sure everything is right with you. Put Yourself First!

V. Young

You never know why certain people come into your life, but everything happens for a reason. If you feel positive vibes, keep them around. If you feel negative vibes, remove them from your life. And that goes for family also! You can't change who your family is, but you can choose whether you want to be bothered with them or not. You just might not want them around you because of the negative energy that they bring. And that's okay! Because your life is very important! And being happy and content is priceless! So always choose who you want to stay in your life!

V. Young

Live your life and always remain true to yourself! Care less about what others may think of you, because you should only be paying attention to the opinions that matter.

V. Young

To Adidja Azim Palmer: You drive me absolutely crazy, but I wouldn't trade you in for anyone or anything in the world. #destiny

To The Main Three Motivators In My Life: One of the main reasons why I work so hard and I don't ever give up, is because the three of you depend on me. And I don't ever want to let you down. Mommy loves you.

Keep It To Yourself

I went over everything, and it didn't make any sense. It
never added up, because what you did just wasn't right
I asked you over and over again what went wrong, because
for my relationship, I was ready to fight!

I begged you to let me know why it happened that way
You refused to respond, you had nothing to say

Now you want to meet with me and you want to take
me out
You said that you want to explain what the break up was
all about

It's not up to you to decide when to tell. I wonder why you
thought that was how it should go
You owe it to the person that you hurt, to tell them when
they want to know

I closed that chapter of my life, and it's put away like a
book on a shelf
I'm good, and you're too late. I no longer want to know!
SO KEEP IT TO YOURSELF!

Am I Not Normal?

Am I not normal, because I just don't care?
Am I not normal, because I'm not interested in feelings you want to share?

Am I not normal because I don't have an ounce of sympathy in my heart for you?
I'm lost, didn't I already forgive? What more do you want me to do?

Am I not normal because you tell me all your pitiful stories, and I still don't feel sorry for you?
You thought the grass was greener until you found out that she didn't even know that one plus one equals two

Am I not normal because I just want you to leave me alone?
I don't want you hanging around by my house, and I don't want you to text or call my phone

Am I not normal because I completely erased you from my heart and my mind? You're the past now and I learned to let go.
I feel no type of emotion, just in a blank state when it comes to you. And to think we were once a couple, no one would ever know

Am I not normal because I JUST DON'T FEEL SORRY FOR YOU? I don't feel your pain AND I CANNOT help you!

If you would have tested her out before you left me, then you would have known that she didn't have that glue

Am I not normal? No I'm not because people like you make people like me this way

Listen, I was down and I had to pick myself up! I don't hate you. And I wish you well. But we're done! SO LEAVE ME ALONE! And I have nothing more to say!

They Don't Know

I wrote this poem so many years ago, this is when I officially felt the struggles of what it was like being a single parent, it was so hard, and although I came a long way, its still not easy, but definitely much much better now.

They don't know everything that I have to go through
All they know is that mommy takes care of business and she does what she has to do

Sometimes I'm so sore and tired and in so much pain
Still have to go out and work, whether the sun is shining or it's pouring down rain

Everyone compliments my smile, they think I'm so happy and carefree. Why should I let emotion show?
I'm one step away from a breakdown but my business is my business, and it's not for everyone to know

The struggle is real, there's no doubt
But what's obvious isn't always obvious. So why let it out?

No one can walk in my shoes, and sometimes I can't even recognize my own feet
They're so swollen and they hurt so bad, because I'll walk to save that money, in order to make ends meet

I don't have time to feel sorry for myself when all I hear
is "I'm hungry, when's dinner?"
And while they're setting the table and I'm fixing the
plates, I feel like such a winner

To watch them eat and see the smile on their face
Priceless moments like that, I definitely can't erase

They don't know everything that I have to go through
All they know is that mommy takes care of business and
she does what she has to do

Adidja Azim Palmer

You're #1, you run this, and the haters always fail when they try to bring you down
They're mad because you're The King and only you alone hold the crown

Unstoppable, strong, unmatched, diligent, versatile; And those are just a few words to describe you
No one has accomplished what you have and they can't even dream about doing what you do

Instead of them paying close attention in your class
They chose to envy and execrate, so they didn't learn, and they didn't pass

Competition is non-existent because you put all of them to shame
Of course they know they can't win, but they won't eat if they don't call your name

You're the reason why they don't have to collect bottles and cans
And honestly speaking, those are your real hardcore number one fans

I can never say this enough, but it's an honor to call someone like you my friend
And you already know, that I'm in this with you for life, until the very end!

What Is This?????

Sometimes you act distant like you don't even care
Am I bothered? That, I choose not to share

Well it's obvious if I'm talking about it, anyone can see
I just don't want to be labeled as a nuisance and I don't want you to leave

At times I feel like we have something special, and drama is what I try not to bring
But sometimes I get to thinking, and I just wonder if you tell everyone the same thing

I keep contradicting myself when it comes to you
I'm constantly doing things that I said I'd never do

Never liked anyone to crowd me, always wanted my space, what can I say?
Yet when it comes to you, I wish I could hear from you every single day

Not trying to stress you out, these are just some things that I wanted to mention
Who would have ever thought that I'd actually long for someone's attention

This is the most puzzling experience I've ever been through, I can't even lie
I can honestly say that I love you, but why?

Fascination vs. obsession, same difference, according to what I believe
You're allowed to have a dissimilar view, it's how you see it, and what you perceive

I guess this is what destiny feels like, although at times it gets very strange
Well, I love you, and I can't control it, so I'm here, and that's definitely not going to change!

Lost And Confused

I'm lost and confused, what can I say
Trying to figure out why life is a certain way

Although in deep thought, I never have doubt
Just need to know what this attraction and obsession is
all about

It's more than obvious that this is something very real
No one is in my mind or my body, and they can't tell me
what I feel

People catch feelings because I have no interest at all in
anyone here
According to my zodiac, I desire what's far away, as
opposed to what's near

When I eat, I often wonder if you're eating too
People can say this, and they can say that, but only you
know what you deal with and have to go through

Sometimes I can't go to sleep at night because you'll pop
up in my head
It's like I'll feel your hidden pain, and I get sad, so I get
up out the bed

Life is a journey, I definitely agree with you on that one, you have to be tough, and you have to be strong
Your haters are so miserable and stressed out because they just don't understand how you've managed to stay relevant for so long

They say he's down! He's out! This has to be his downfall, yes! This is it!
Then they turn on the radio, and as always, their celebrations are short-lived, because they realize that you've just released another hit

The amount of endurance that you possess seems very abnormal, and it's a mystery how you remain standing tall
Some people need to observe and take notes because you are The Teacha, you are The WorlBoss, and without question, you are The King Of The Dancehall

It'll be so nice when you walk out those doors and you'll finally be free
Even though I'm very patient, I'm also excited, because that's something I can't wait to see

Until then I'm lost and confused, what can I say
Just trying to figure out why life is a certain way

You're Stuck With Me

Why do you insist on treating me so cold?
If I we're in front of you, would you be this
bold?

I've never dealt with this type of attitude and behavior
before
Your actions leave me speechless and curious, and I want
to see more

I'm sorry, I've learned my lesson and I'm ready to be a
good girl now
I'll be quiet and listen, just teach me how

You get so mad at me instead of just telling me what I
did wrong
Since you don't let me know, I probably keep doing it,
and that's why this silent treatment always lasts for so long

When I see you, I plan on holding you tight and I'm not
letting go, so let's see if I get my way
Will you embrace me? What will you do? Do you plan
on pushing me away?

I love how your voice puts me to sleep every single night
I'm under your spell, I'm at your beck and call. Please,
let's not fight

I'm very private, I can be your best kept secret, I know how to lay low
But if you need me to stand by your side, I'll be right there! Front and Center! You Already know!

You said that it was destiny from the start, and that's what it will always be
Your words are already spoken! And for that reason alone, I'm smiling! Because you should know that you're stuck with me!

I Know You Miss Me

I know you miss me just as much as I miss you
Are you really gonna sit there and act like
what we have isn't true?

Since when did you want me to be quiet, I'm outspoken
but always kind
And now you start to get mad because I speak my mind

Many people won't tell you anything because they act like
they're scared of you
But you know good and well that I'm going to voice my
opinion about some of the things that you do

Then you get upset and you ignore me, just let it out!
You're allowed to vent!
Instead you start carrying feelings! It's okay, you don't
have to like my comment

We clicked because we're both crazy, it's like you were sent
from up above
And no matter what we go through, we're supposed to
work it out, because it's all love

I know you miss me just as much as I miss you
Come on now! Are you really gonna sit there and act like
what we have isn't true?

You're So Different

You're so different, but you're worth it
Never had a friendship like this before, so I
refuse to quit

You pull me in but then you try to push me away
Stop the light switch activity because I'm here to stay

You can't possibly think that I'm about to be added to the
list of people that gave up on you
I'm here, so get use to it because as far as my resilience
goes, you have no clue

I'll admit it's not easy having a friend like you
Especially when you do mean things and you don't think
them through

No matter how weird this gets, I see you and you see me
And that's the way it will always be

I know you can't believe it, but yes it's real
And even though you're obdurate at times, you still can't
hide how you really feel

People come into each other's lives for a reason, and most
of the time it can't be explained or figured out
No worries, just let it flow. Because this is solid, without
question and without doubt!

You're so different, but you're worth it
Never had a friendship like this before, so I refuse to quit

Reality

Sometimes it's so fun living in this imaginary
world as if we're the only ones who exist
Then here comes reality, just messing everything
up with that unwanted twist

We're very cool, we flirt, always good convo, and we have
lots of fun!
It will stay right there though because we all know that
you can't have just one

I will never try to change you... I accept you for who you are
At the same time though, you can't blame me for wishing
on a star

It's an honor, and it's a pleasure to have someone in my
life like you
I don't care how many people I know, there is no
comparison, and respect will always be given because
it's due

I'll admit that I often have inappropriate thoughts when
it comes to you, but so what!
Look at everything you do to me, you're a slick one, but
my legs still remain shut

You probably feel that if it weren't for the circumstances they would have been spread open a long time ago
Maybe you're right, but maybe you're wrong, maybe you don't need to know

There are times though, when you speak I feel like I need some type of shield or protection
Because I'll drift off in a trance and be so drawn in, that I'll even consider being part of your collection

You make me feel really special and that's why I get so caught up in your spell
The way you have me acting sometimes, I even have to question if I'm well

It's just crazy how it just seems so real at times, as if we actually live as one
Then I open my eyes, I'm awake, my senses are back, and the dream is done

Sometimes it's so fun living in this imaginary world as if we're the only ones who exist
Then here comes reality, just messing everything up with that unwanted twist

Emma a.k.a. Emily

I'm so glad that I have a friend like you
Whatever I have going on I know that all I have to do is
pick up the phone and you'll help see me through

There have been times when I was so upset, eyes watery,
tears ready to fall
But once we started talking, we'd laugh so much and I'd
actually forget the reason I made the call

I'm allergic to fake people. I only welcome positive energy,
and loyalty is a must! So who I choose to keep around me
is not a game
No matter what, our friendship was one of the most
consistent things in my life because it always stayed the
same

I'm labeled as being tough and strong, and that may be
true. But I'm human and you know that. You've been
with me for the happy times as well as the sad times when
I cried
I've been through so many things, and some are
unbelievable, but I couldn't even make them up if I tried

And your dedication and loyalty means so much because
I know more often than not, you're going through your
own thing

But everything will be okay soon! Next year will be here before we know it! And a special shout out goes to KAREEM!

I'm often caught up and busy, I live a hectic life as you know, and it's always something to do
But I decided to take this time out to tell you once again, that I'm so glad to have a friend like you!

Shawanda

I remember that day when I wasn't feeling well and you called, but I just wanted to be left alone
You were so worried about me, and no matter what, you just wouldn't get off the phone

I still appreciate it now, and I although it didn't seem like it, I appreciated it then
I know I've told you before, but I'm saying thank you again

Stories were created about you and lies were told. And so much shade was thrown in your direction.
But whenever I saw you, all I felt was positive energy, excellent vibes, and some sort of connection

They'd smile in your face but always had something negative to say about you
It's called being phony, so that was very easy for them to do

They'd entertain anyone that he brought around and always interfered with your relationship. They did all of that because you were a threat
He needs to grow up and think for himself. And put people in their place when it comes to you. If not, that'll be his biggest regret.

You're far from desperate and very smart
But my mind kept telling me that from the start

If I would have listened to them I would have thought
that you were just one big dummy
I'm glad I really got to know you. Now you're acknowledged
and they aren't, isn't life funny?

Tut

Whether you know it or not, you helped me get through a really rough time in my life, and I just wanted to say thank you
You checked on me almost every day, you gave words of encouragement, and that's not something you had to do

Sometimes I'd be so mad and stressed out and I just didn't know which way to turn or which way to go
Then I'd communicate with you, and you'd say something that would just make me think. And then all of a sudden, I'd know.

You counsel so many people in there, and I'm glad that you're my counselor too
You need to know that I'm grateful, and I appreciate all that you do

There were times when you made me smile when I just wanted to cry
You'd remind me that because of how I'm built, they can never break me no matter how hard they try

They say that blood is thicker than water, and although it's obvious, I still question whether or not it's true
Because if that's the case, how come as far as siblings go, the only one that I acknowledge is you

When you said that I give you inspiration and my words give you strength, I was lost and didn't know what to say
Because coming from someone like you, that really meant a lot, and it definitely made my day

And for you to have said that, I knew it was true
So I take great pride in knowing, that just as you help me I help you too

I reside in Queens, but BROOKLYN WE SAY!
That's where I was born! That's What I know! ENY ALL DAY! EVERYDAY!

I can never mention East New York without mentioning you
Just as you respect me, you already know that I respect you too

We communicate quite often so I'm not gonna make this too long
Thanks again for everything! And you know how we always end it, STAY STRONG!

Family

There was a poem that I wrote called Family, and it was supposed to be on this page. I decided not to publish it, because some things are better left unsaid. I hope you enjoyed the other poems though, and I thank you so much for purchasing my book. It's appreciated.

V. Young

If anyone wants to leave any comments or feedback, feel free to write the author. Contact information is below.

V. Young
117-01 127 Street, Suite 829
South Ozone Park, NY 11420

Email: v.youngdbk@gmail.com

Printed in the United States
By Bookmasters